This book is a gift to:

Joyce

Message:

WHAT A DELIGHT YOU ARE!!
IT'S A PLEASURE HAVING YOU
ATTEND "JAMES"

Date:

4/30/12

From:

Jan

Blessings from God for Women

© 2012 Christian Art Gifts, RSA
Christian Art Gifts Inc., IL, USA

Designed by Christian Art Gifts

Images used under license from Shutterstock.com

Printed in China

ISBN 978-1-77036-642-8

12 13 14 15 16 17 18 19 20 21 – 10 9 8 7 6 5 4 3 2 1

Blessings
from God
for Women

Karen Moore

christian
art gifts®

Dedication:

I'm grateful to the people who have blessed
my life over and over again.
Thanks especially to some of my dearest friends:
Bev Luedecke, Douglas De Ford, Stan McClure,
Betty Powell and Tom Kapella.

You bless my life!

Blessings Abound

God sees you. God knows you.
God blesses you.

Sometimes it feels like blessings fall upon you like raindrops on the upturned faces of velvety purple flowers. Other times, it feels like you're wilting, dragging your sagging leaves anywhere to find supportive root systems, or to simply confirm you're still sitting in God's window box.

May this little book inspire your heart and awaken you to the blessings God has for you every day. Before you even get out of bed in the morning, He's been busy planning and preparing new opportunities for you to experience life, discover new areas of growth, and inspire change. He wants you to recognize all that He has for you before your feet hit the floor. Walk with Him and let the sunshine in. See where His love carries you to make this day better.

Blessings from God for Women is for you, a woman of great worth, purposely created and designed, lavishly blessed, and a woman after God's own heart. In His garden, you're a delicate flower of great beauty.

> *The meek will inherit the land*
> *and enjoy peace and prosperity.*
> Psalm 37:11 NIV

A Blessed Thought

May God give you ...

For every storm a rainbow,

for every tear a smile,

For every care a promise

and a blessing in each trial ...

For every problem life brings,

a faithful friend to share,

For every sigh a song of joy

and an answer for each prayer.

Adapted from an Irish Blessing

May You Be Blessed to Be a Blessing at Home

> Where we love is home, home that our feet may leave, but not our hearts.
>
> Oliver Wendell Holmes

From our tender beginning, from the womb where we grew and were nurtured to become who we are today, God blessed the place we call home. He provided for our well-being, making sure we had everything we needed to survive and grow strong.

In the best scenario, He placed us in a family where we could be held and loved and tutored. If we didn't have a home environment that was ideal, God strengthened us and kept watch over us so we could someday stand on our own, become more sensitive to life, and understand His call to us more fully.

Ideally, His blessing tied home and heart together, creating a space that brought us a gentle longing to seek more of Him. Being part of a family, no matter how we define it, is God's way of giving us a place to start on the journey to become our best selves. After all, we're each uniquely designed.

God Put His Designer Label on You

Home is definitely where we can hang our hearts, and it's our place to safely spend time figuring out who we are.

Now that we're adults, some of us love to create a comforting space where we retreat in our favorite bathrobe, savoring our latte in a quiet nook with the book *du jour*. Others jump into the day, running the race in the outside world and counting the minutes until we can heave a deep sigh in our easy chair when we find our way home again.

We're blessed to rest and renew our energy, replenish our daily bread and reconnect with the One who protects us and cares for us. Home is our sanctuary, the sacred place that gives us all we need to strive to share whatever is left of us with others.

It is where we learn to be givers and receivers, turning on the light so we can see the world around us. Home is the refueling station for your energy and your spirit. God bless your home!

God is more anxious to bestow
His blessings on us than we are to receive them.

St. Augustine

Blessings to Share ...

May you soak up all the goodness the Lord has for you right now and wash away the cares of yesterday. Make a fresh start with whatever you do today and be refueled and re-energized to step out into the world fully blessed.

St. Augustine said, "One loving soul sets another on fire." Your light is meant to shine today, meant to show someone else the way. You've been blessed so that you may become a greater blessing to those around you.

Do you want your days to matter? Want your moments to be memorable, to stand out? If you do then take note. You'll have the best memories and the best interactions of your life when your intention is to serve, to give, and to make this world a better place. You matter! What you do matters!

God needs your smile, your kind words, and your energy to create goodness. God needs you to be the blessing. That's a fact!

Charles Spurgeon reminded us that the work of one person, one person willing to step out and jump in, makes a difference. He said, "The greatest works are done by the ones. The hundreds do not often do much, the companies never; it is the units, the single individuals, who are the power and the might. Individual effort is, after all, the grand thing."

How Can You Bless Others?

What's the most effective way then to be a woman who blesses others?

Perhaps this thought from Thomas à Kempis helps:

First put yourself at peace, and then you may better make others be at peace. A peaceful and patient woman is of more profit to herself and to others, too, than a learned woman who has no peace.

We're intelligent, strong, and learned women. What we may not be are women at peace with ourselves. Perhaps the key is to find our way to peace, that inner witness of truth and strength that gives us the opportunity to bless those around us.

In John 14:27 in the *Amplified Bible* we read, "Peace I leave with you: My [own] peace I now give and bequeath to you. Not as the world gives do I give to you. Do not let your hearts be troubled, neither let them be afraid." [Stop allowing yourselves to be agitated and disturbed; and do not permit yourselves to be fearful and intimidated and cowardly and unsettled.]

It's not easy to be at peace, but it's possible. It's not always easy to be a woman of blessing and grace, but it's possible. The world needs the possibility we bring when we can do these things. It's a precious part of our calling.

Blessings to Share ...

Every time I create new
possibilities for myself or someone else,
I create blessings. Blessings open doors
to new ideas and release my heart
to experience

joy
and
peace.

Blessed [of God] is he who
blesses you
[who prays for and contributes
to your welfare.]

Numbers 24:9 AMP

Blessed to Be a Blessing

Light Your Own Candle First

The image of letting your light shine is a powerful one. Couple that with the thought of being a candle, created to share the light, and it gets even stronger.

Perhaps when we find ourselves complaining about the things of the world it's because we've let our own candle go out. We've forgotten the power of blessing and the joy that we experience when we share that light. Let's relight our candle and those of others and light up the whole world.

Pass the Torch!

George Bernard Shaw said this about candles: "Life is no brief candle to me. It is a sort of splendid torch which I have got a hold of for the moment, and I want to make it burn as brightly as possible before handing it on to future generations."

When your candle is lit, or your torch is aflame, you can show others the way. Your heart grows bigger, rounder, and softer and everything in your spirit seeks the greater good. When your brain is engaged in such a way, you become life giving and life affirming and your spirit enters a condition of perpetual peace. What warmth your inner light brings! What a blessing it is!

How far that little candle throws his beams!
So shines a good deed in a naughty world.

William Shakespeare

A Prayer for You

May the Lord bless you and keep you, and may He shine His brightest smile on your heart today, showing you all He has for you, revealing His love in brand-new ways. May God light your candle of love and bless your life in all you do for Him.

Amen.

Blessings at Home for You and Those You Love

There is no doubt that it is around the family and the home that all the greatest virtues, the most dominating virtues of human society, are created, strengthened and maintained.

Winston Churchill

God knew we needed a sense of family and community in order to understand one another's needs, to understand compassion and how to offer encouragement. He knew the best place for us to learn these things was in the heart of a good home, with a family who loved us just as He had made us. We were blessed by our families and are still blessed by all those who care for and nurture us so we can be strengthened and made ready to serve whenever He calls us.

A nurturing family makes a tremendous difference in how we connect with life, how we work with others and how we manage the roller coaster experience of each day. You are a role model to others and to your family. You're an example of God's love to everyone who sees you and interacts with you.

As Mother Teresa noted,

"Love begins at home, and it is not how much we do … but how much love we put in that action."

Love, both tough and tender, and steadfast and growing is the motivation behind all we do, the real essence of who we are. A family tutors us in love and causes us to learn how to put love into action. Those actions become the blessings we can choose to offer as we grow and move beyond that nucleus of home.

The Hug Blessing

The man who turned giving a hug into a profession also turned actions into blessings for countless people. His name was Leo Buscaglia and he reminded us that "Too often we underestimate the power of a touch, a smile, a kind word, a listening ear, an honest compliment, or the smallest act of caring, all of which have the potential to turn a life around."

It is in the small things that we learn the most about how to handle the big things. This is truly where actions speak louder than words.

For You and Your Family

Each one of us is special,
Created by God's hand,
Strengthened by His love
To become all that He had planned.

He gave us gifts of kindness,
Wisdom, truth and grace,
Protecting us through trials
And the things He knew we'd face.

He made us one big family,
And hoped we each would bless
All those we meet along the way
With gifts of happiness.

You Are Blessed to Create a Home Where Everybody Thrives

"Feelings of worth can flourish only in an atmosphere where individual differences are appreciated, mistakes are tolerated, communication is open, and rules are flexible - the kind of atmosphere that is found in a nurturing family."

Virginia Satir

There's No Place Like Your Home

Unless the Lord builds the house,
the builders labor in vain. Psalm 127:1 NIV

There's no place like home ... like your home, that is. It may have quirks and questions. It may leave you wondering the why or what or the how and when of things that happen. It may not even serve you very well at times, but no matter how imperfectly you were raised, you may have a sense that there's really no place like home.

Oh sure, there are crazy times when you don't understand the people there. You may not always like the people there, but you have a very clear picture in your heart and mind that somehow those people are yours, the ones who know you and welcome you back no matter what. Even when you go astray, they are there. You call them your family.

Blessings to Share ...

Today, I am grateful to my family for all that they do to support me, all the ways they lend a hand or help me think things through. I honor them as the ones God designed for me to love and to learn from, to inspire me and to challenge me to become more.

The Prodigal Son Lives On

Remember the story of the Prodigal Son, the one who squandered his father's wealth, living a carefree, thoughtless life until it all disappeared with his last shekel?

Finally, the son suffered the misery of what he had done and decided to return home, knowing he might not be welcomed back again, but determined to do whatever it took to be back in his father's embrace.

In the days and nights it took for him to make the long journey home, you can imagine how heavy his heart must have been. Think about how often he had to rehearse the speech he planned to make to change his father's heart enough to allow him back in the door. He even thought of becoming one of his father's servants, because he would do anything, simply to be home again.

Nearing the house, coming within range, the son was spotted by a servant and his father was told that a traveler was coming. When the father realized that it was his own dear son, the one he had given up for dead and was now returning to him, he threw down his tools and began to run. He ran with such joy to embrace his boy, his precious one, the one he had never dreamed of holding again. He hugged him and shouted for the servants to prepare a welcoming feast. His son was alive and well.

Blessings to Share ...

I am the certainty, the smile of welcome. Let me run to bless my loved ones with welcoming arms. Let me run to them even before they know I am coming their way.

Prodigal Sons and Daughters

We've each been prodigal sons and daughters. We've experienced some distance from our family, some kind of isolation from those we love. We may even wander a bit too far sometimes and wonder whether we can truly ever go back. The truth is that we can and God prepares the blessing, the opportunity for us to return with open arms and open hearts.

We're always welcomed home again. This story serves as our example that we're welcomed back home every time we look to Him with humble and contrite hearts. God wants us to remember that each time someone we love wanders away, each time we find ourselves going astray, each time we begin to wonder where home might be He receives us as soon as we come to His door. He's designed us to welcome each other back as well.

God keeps the door open, blessing us with
experience so we can forgive ourselves or
understand others in our families who may have
wandered a bit too far and need a way back.

A Blessed Thought

When twilight drops
her curtain down and
pins it with a star,
remember that you have a friend
though she may wander far.

Luke's story of the Prodigal Son is our story too. Take a look at it once again.

The Prodigal Son from Luke 15:11-24:

Jesus said, "There was a certain man who had two sons; and the younger of them said to his father, Father, give me the part of the property that falls [to me]. And he divided the estate between them.

And not many days after that, the younger son gathered up all that he had and journeyed into a distant country, and there he wasted his fortune in reckless and loose [from restraint] living.

And when he had spent all he had, a mighty famine came upon that country, and he began to fall behind and be in want.

So he went and forced (glued) himself upon one of the citizens of that country, who sent him into his fields to feed hogs.

And he would gladly have fed on and filled his belly with the carob pods that the hogs were eating, but [they could not satisfy his hunger and] nobody gave him anything [better].

Then when he came to himself, he said, How many hired

servants of my father have enough food, and [even food] to spare, but I am perishing (dying) here of hunger!

I will get up and go to my father, and I will say to him, Father, I have sinned against heaven and in your sight.

I am no longer worthy to be called your son; [just] make me like one of your hired servants.

So he got up and came to his [own] father. But while he was still a long way off, his father saw him and was moved with pity and tenderness [for him]; and he ran and embraced him and kissed him [fervently].

And the son said to him, Father, I have sinned against heaven and in your sight; I am no longer worthy to be called your son [I no longer deserve to be recognized as a son of yours]!

But the father said to his bond servants, Bring quickly the best robe (the festive robe of honor) and put it on him; and give him a ring for his hand and sandals for his feet.

And bring out that [wheat-]fattened calf and kill it; and let us revel and feast and be happy and make merry, because this my son was dead and is alive again; he was lost and is found! And they began to revel and feast and make merry" (AMP).

Lord, it isn't always easy to find a way home again, heart-broken, wretched, disappointed with our choices and the outcome of our decisions. It isn't easy, but it's so gratifying to know that in spite of all we've done, Your love shines out in the darkness beckoning us to come home again ... open arms, all is forgiven. Thank You for the gift of Your love. Amen.

The Welcome Blessing

There's nothing quite as beautiful
When you've traveled someplace far
As seeing the sweet light of home
With the door left just ajar.
It's a beacon in the wilderness
Much more than window dressing
It's the light that welcomes you again
And fills your heart with blessing.

Pass the Blessing Along

Have you had a kindness shown?
Pass it on;
It wasn't given for you alone,
Pass it on;
Let it travel down the years,
Let it wipe another's tears,
'Til in heaven the deed appears –
Pass it on.

Henry Burton, adapted from *Pass It On*

Blessings to Share ...

No matter where I go today, God will lead me safely on. He will keep me in His care and bring my heart home again. He will wrap me in His blanket of peace and bless me with the courage to shine my humble light wherever any darkness appears.

The moment we break faith with one another, the sea engulfs us and the light goes out.

James Baldwin

The Blessing of Words

It's not always easy to remember that what you say matters, especially to the people in your family. Your words can cut like a knife or heal an aching heart. Your kind and thoughtful words make a difference. Words motivated by anger or pride can hurt for a lifetime. Never doubt that the choices you make and the words you speak may echo through the mind of your loved ones for years to come. Be careful then. Words are powerful! How can your words be a blessing today?

Sowing the Good Words

George Matthew Adams put it this way: "It's what each of us sows, and how, that gives to us character and prestige. Seeds of kindness, goodwill, and human understanding, planted in fertile soil, spring up into deathless friendships, big deeds of worth, and a memory that will not soon fade out. We are all sowers of seeds – and let us never forget it."

Sowing the Seeds of Blessing

- A home is blessed each time a hug is shared.

- A kind word at the right moment is a blessing to the heart.

- A woman's family is held together by her wisdom.
  Proverbs 14:1 CEV

- Each time you recount a blessing, it blesses you again.

- You can never be too grateful for your blessings.

- You must know that blessings have wings.

- The hand of blessing is always open.

- God blessed you to bless others.

- Out of your kindness, blessings grow.

- Your words are mustard seeds of blessing.

Good Words to Share

When you think about the words that make a difference to you, they probably have to do with encouragement or love. They are words that remind you that you're unique and beautiful and a gift to others and they give you every reason to smile again, to shine your light once more. The words that assure you that you're not alone and that others are walking beside you, ready to help, ready to listen, ready to lend a hand, are the ones that give you strength.

The words that say, "I love you just the way you are, and I accept you with all your craziness, all your incredibleness, all your amazing ways of being", are the words that bless you. Those words heal you.

Your only job is to remember how much you need those words and then to give those same words away. That's right! The very thing you need is the thing you must give away. The more you give away words of love and encouragement, the more opportunity you have to be a blessing. Your words make a difference at home, with your family, and in the neighborhood.

Blessings to Share ...

Today, I will make a difference to a stranger, sharing a kind word or smile. Today, I will make a difference to a friend, encouraging and supporting thoughts and dreams. Today, I will make a difference to myself, believing that I am blessed to be a blessing.

A Word of Prayer

Lord, help us to remember that each word from our lips has the power for good or the power for destruction. Remind us that we are Your ambassadors of goodwill, speaking for You in all we do.

Amen.

You Are a Blessing to the Neighborhood

Women have a knack for being neighborly. They visit a newcomer with a batch of home-baked cookies. They share a smile or a conversation on the front lawn, extending the hand of friendship, opening the door of kindness.

Good neighbors are a blessing

and God has definite ideas about how

neighbors should be treated.

One example for us comes from Proverbs:

"Never walk away from someone who deserves help; your hand is God's hand for that person. Don't tell your neighbor 'Maybe some other time' or 'Try me tomorrow' when the money's right there in your pocket. Don't figure ways of taking advantage of your neighbor when he's sitting there trusting and unsuspecting."

Proverbs 3:26-27 MSG

A New Rule:

Make it a rule, and **pray to God** to help you to keep it, never, if possible, to lie down at night without being able to say: "I have made one human being at least a little wiser, or a little happier, or at least a little better **this day**."

Charles Kingsley

So What Happened to Being a Good Neighbor?

Being neighborly has become a lost art, a vague memory of years gone by. Maybe you remember your grandmother's porch where people sat and talked about world events and life's special moments. They intentionally created a sense of community and they blessed each other in the process.

It's easy today to become isolated, cocooned in our own living space, and we can get pretty good at keeping the world out. We may have actually forgotten how to be neighbors, caught in urban sprawl and high-rise isolation booths. The more we disconnect from each other, the more we experience the polar opposite of what human friendship and family is all about. We were designed for community. God wants neighbors to bless each other's lives.

So What Does it Mean to Be a Good Neighbor?

Here's a short list of possibilities:

- Don't let anyone around you become invisible, touch their lives.
- Honor each other's boundaries.
- Respect each other's choices.
- Lend a hand, if possible, without even being asked.
- Say hello, wave and smile as you pass by.
- Say please and thank you.
- Acknowledge the life situations and circumstances that may be out of your neighbor's control and even out of yours, and offer comfort.
- Let no one remain a stranger.
- Keep the light on.
- Remember that we're all a lot more alike than we are different from each other.
- Pray.
- Celebrate the joys of relationship and connection.
- Keep a neighborhood watch. Remember you're all God's family.
- Don't isolate yourself from others. No need to hide.
- Be the first to offer a hand of friendship.
- Be the first to forgive a small misunderstanding.

Keep adding to this list. You already know how to be a good neighbor, so pass on the blessing.

A Sense of Community

I am of the opinion that my life belongs to the whole community and as long as I live, it is my privilege to do for it whatever I can. I want to be thoroughly used up when I die, for the harder I work the more I live.

George Bernard Shaw

Blessings to Share ...

May I create opportunities in my neighborhood to bless people's lives in new ways. As I do, I realize the blessing moves forward, then back to me again, freely spreading the light of God's love, circling the community with a sense of warm energy and new connection.

A Blessed Thought

Goethe said that there are nine conditions that contribute to contented living:

1. Health enough to make work a pleasure;
2. Wealth enough to support your needs;
3. Strength enough to battle with difficulties and forsake them;
4. Grace enough to confess your sins and overcome them;
5. Patience enough to toil until some good is accomplished;

6. Charity enough to see some good in your neighbor;
7. Love enough to move you to be useful and helpful to others;
8. Faith enough to make real the things of God;
9. Hope enough to remove all anxious fears concerning the future.

As you consider all the ways that your life is meant to be a blessing, all the ways that you have enough, may you work toward that gentle condition of peace and contentment that heartfelt giving brings. It will indeed give sweetness and life to your days.

A Prayer for You

May God bless you so that you always find that you have enough; enough hope and strength, enough love and charity, enough patience and joy. May your health exceed your wealth and your faith offer the foundation that makes all things worthwhile.

Amen.

The Rule of Neighborly Friendship

The rule of friendship means there should be mutual sympathy between them, each supplying what the other lacks and trying to benefit the other, always using friendly and sincere words.

Cicero

Won't You Be My Neighbor?

If you grew up with Fred Rogers, you might still find yourself singing his opening song from his children's TV show about "wanting to have a neighbor just like you, wanting to live in a neighborhood with you," asking you to simply be his neighbor. The simplicity of the song and the thought it evokes has its own charm, but the idea is actually powerful.

A sense of community serves to create friends and neighbors, giving them a place to belong, a place to serve, and a place to bless others. The invitation is open to make friends and neighbors of everyone you meet.

No one may forsake his neighbor when he is in trouble. Everybody is under obligation to help and support his neighbor as he would himself like to be helped.

Martin Luther

A Neighborly Word from Scripture

"Summing up: Be agreeable, be sympathetic, be loving, be compassionate, be humble. That goes for all of you, no exceptions. No retaliation. No sharp-tongued sarcasm. Instead, bless — that's your job, to bless. You'll be a blessing and also get a blessing. Whoever wants to embrace life and see the day fill up with good, here's what you do: Say nothing evil or hurtful; snub evil and cultivate good; run after peace for all you're worth. God looks on all this with approval, listening and responding well to what He's asked; but He turns His back on those who do evil things." 1 Peter 3:9-12 MSG

Blessings to Share ...

I am a good neighbor, ready to act when someone is struggling, ready to listen when needs arise, ready to give in any way that lifts the spirit of someone near to me. It's my day to shine as a good neighbor.

A Prayer for Neighbors

Lord, kindly bless my neighbors
And keep them in Your care,
Help us all reach out in joy.
And connect us through this prayer.

Amen.

While the **spirit of neighborliness** was important on the frontier because **neighbors** were so few, it is even more **important** now because **our neighbors** are so many.

Lady Bird Johnson

Blessed to Be a Blessing at Work

You work all the time. When you're working for yourself or others, you may lose sight of the opportunity to be blessed or to pass along that blessing to those who work with you. Even at work the intention is never just for you to succeed, or to have more at the expense of others. The intention is for you to succeed and share that success with others in every way possible.

How You're a Blessing at Work

- You're a blessing when you recognize someone else and give them credit for the work they do.

- You're a blessing when you see a person struggling to accomplish something that is out of their area of expertise and you offer a solution.

- You're a blessing when you find the right kind of help to make a job more effective and rewarding.

- You're a blessing when you acknowledge the presence of those who work behind the scenes, the ones whose work may not appear to affect your immediate job in any way.

- You're a blessing in the workplace in many ways and that job is never done.

Jonas Salk said, "The reward for work well done is the opportunity to do more."

In any case, we can all do more for each other wherever we work and in whatever way we utilize our particular talents. You weren't given your gifts only to hoard them, in fact, you're never to hoard them. The idea is to remember that you're a force for good, a part of the whole group, and what you do for others is needed if any hope exists to make blessings a normal part of living.

Blessings to Share ...

I can do something today that will inspire someone I work with, or simply make their job easier. It makes me smile to bring strength to my friends and co-workers.

We Always Have Work to Do

If our work is to love God with our whole heart and mind, and to love our neighbors as ourselves, then we're always busy. If we do our work well, then blessings are an integral part of all we do, both the ones bestowed on us and the ones we share. How can we be more intentional then about passing along the blessings, the talents designed by our Maker for our use and intended to benefit God's children?

Perhaps part of the answer lies in remembering who the people are that you work with each day. Do you really see them?

Past the seeker as he prayed came the crippled and the lame, and the beggar and the beaten. And seeing them ... he cried, "Great God, how is it that a loving Creator can see such things and yet do nothing about them?" God said, "I did do something. I made you."

Anonymous

Luciano de Crescenzo said, "We are each of us angels with only one wing, and we can only fly by embracing one another."

We were made

to do something

and to **embrace**

each other

in the process.

The People You Work with are Friends ... First!

How can we see the people we work with as unique individuals? How can we go beyond our position or some arbitrary title that has been assigned to us by a job, and serve others better?

People we work with are no different than the people we meet in the walkways of life every day. They are simply people like us doing a job, taking care of their families and trying to make sense of life. We don't always see them that way though. We are motivated by the things that attach them to the job. Will they get in the way of our next promotion? Will they give us support on our pet projects? Will they gossip about us? Are they really team players?

One author put it this way, "Regardless of differences, we strive shoulder to shoulder ... Teamwork can be summed up in five short words: 'We believe in each other.'"

It's important to believe in the people you spend a large portion of your day with and this observation is true regardless of whether your team is at home, in a classroom, or a corporate office somewhere. Believing in each other means we don't have to second guess our actions at work and wonder if our best efforts are even worth the risk.

Without meaning to, we may judge ourselves and those in our immediate sphere of influence unfairly. It's good then to listen to the guiding voice within our spirits that works every minute to give us a more abundant life. It's that same voice that blesses us so we can pass our gifts along with grace and charity.

I appreciate this piece, re-crafted from another writer some time ago. It echoes the sentiments of a popular song performed by Martina McBride called *Do It Anyway!*

See how these nuggets of blessing resonate with you:

- People can be unreasonable and unpredictable and self-centered, they can be forgetful and ungrateful ... love them anyway!

- If you volunteer to do good things simply to be a blessing, people may question your motives and tell you you're not thinking clearly ... do good things anyway; be a blessing!

- If you become a success in business or in life, you may threaten your friends and your enemies alike. You may cause them to have to re-evaluate their own current life position ... become a success anyway!

- If you're honest and vulnerable, people may take advantage of you, they may manipulate you even more for their own gain, totally missing the beauty of who you are and the blessing you bring to their lives ... be honest and vulnerable anyway!

- If you dream of great things, but only get to do good things, you may question your dreams ... but keep dreaming of great things anyway.

- If you try hard and win for a moment, you may lose in the end, you may have to start over, you may not realize the blessing of this effort immediately, in fact, you may never realize the true blessing of your efforts ... try hard anyway!

- If you love with your whole heart, you may still get your heart broken, you may be led astray or you may generously give to those who do not even deserve what you offer ... love with your whole heart anyway!

- If you pray to God, you may have days go by without hearing His voice or getting any answers, you may wonder if He even knows you are there ... pray to God anyway!

- If you do your best, give generously and love the people around you, you may never know just what it meant to others ... but be grateful ... and be generous and do your best anyway!

Blessings to Share ...

I can do something with my whole heart today.

I can give my best, give generously,

be forgiving and grateful.

I can be these things because I am truly blessed.

We can do no great things,

only small things with great love.

Mother Teresa

It May Take Courage to Be a Blessing

Whatever you have to offer, whatever you can give, there's only one you, called to a purpose, guided by a gracious spirit! **Where your heart guides, blessing resides.** So go on, be your amazing self.

> Do it all! Do it well!
> Do it with love!
> Do it anyway!

As human beings, we share a lot of common ground whatever our world view or our culture or heritage. We want to believe in all that's good, have faith in tomorrow, and strive to make a difference.

We want to feel more connected than separate from the rest of the world, appreciate our uniqueness and our humanity, and in some respects, even remember and safeguard our innocence. We also want to understand how to love each other unconditionally ... how to embrace each other just the way we are, with no hidden agendas, with no need to fix anything ... just loved.

All of these wants and desires take courage. They don't just happen. They take effort and they are the reason we've been equipped to be a blessing to each other.

In the way that is most authentic for you, you need to highlight the good, renew hope, and strengthen your bonds. If you can put a hug in an email or shine a light so someone can see the road ahead a bit better, then that's a worthwhile effort. That's an important mission.

The fact is, we live in a world that has plenty of the dark side. We fumble a lot out there, sometimes even losing our way, because the dark is overbearing and persistent. Social media and instant news gathering have made it harder to stay the course and bring the more positive things to light.

There are two ways
of spreading light –
to be the candle
or the mirror
that reflects it.

Edith Wharton

Blessings to Share ...

I can be the light for someone today. I can stand at the crossroads and help point the way to a richer possibility, reminding them that they have a light within longing to be kindled, ready to ignite the world, and that it is a light placed there by their Heavenly Father who has loved them since the beginning.

Get Out Your Candle

If you have a matchstick or hold up a candle or you have a flashlight and it lights up your thoughts or triggers a positive action in you so others see you in a warmer way, then you have been called. You are an ambassador, ready and spiritually programmed to deliver a kind of divine joyful energy.

Be encouraged to keep beaming your light into the world. Bring joy and genuine warmth and possibility to those around you. Lift the spirits of people in need. Solve problems that give others hope. Point the way and guide the heart and pray heartily. You'll not only be an inspiration, you'll be somebody's miracle.

But if by chance, you're having a gray day, let someone else light the way for you, receive their light, and then simply rest in that presence until your spirits are aglow again.

After all, you are the light of the world.

When Jesus commented about His followers "being the light of the world," He meant it and we need to take that seriously. Of course in His metaphor, we're only the moon, reflecting the light from the Son, but we're in a great position. We know that there's always a light to follow, always a star over Bethlehem.

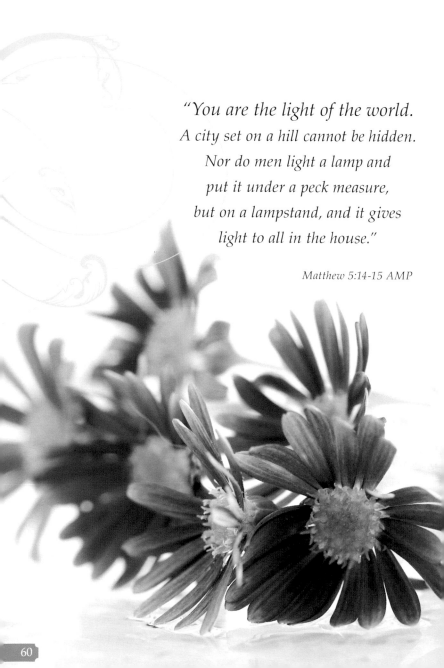

"You are the light of the world.
A city set on a hill cannot be hidden.
Nor do men light a lamp and
put it under a peck measure,
but on a lampstand, and it gives
light to all in the house."

Matthew 5:14-15 AMP

May we all say, "Let there be light. Let there be light in **our hearts** and **our minds** and **our spirits** because we each have gifts to **share** that illuminate the path and get us all home safely." We have been called to **shine** and to be part of the blessing wherever we are. **Shine on!**

The Blessing of Building a Bridge

Did you know we're in the bridge building business? We're civil and spiritual engineers making a way where there isn't one. We fill the gaps and find the spaces where darkness lingers. We're parents building roads to make it easier for our kids to come home when they wander, strengthening their way whatever route they may take. We're spouses creating unshakable connections, braced for life, no matter what we face. We are conduits of joy, changing strangers into friends, foreigners into neighbors, and offering everyone a place of safety as they travel.

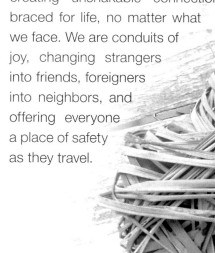

One of my favorite songs performed by The Judds is called *Love Can Build a Bridge*.

The words of the chorus say this:

Love can build a bridge
Between your heart and mine
Love can build a bridge
Don't you think it's time?

How does love build a bridge? Sometimes it lays a foundation of forgiveness. It creates a way over the murky waters of injured pride or misunderstanding and lays the groundwork for peace.

Sometimes it simply shows up, not allowing the silence to become deafening, but reaching out, gently calling until the voices of compassion and reason can be found again.

Sometimes it lightens the load by bringing a sense of humor to a tense moment, offering everyone involved a chance to see more clearly and find the way back to each other.

No matter what tool it devises, love, or forgiveness, or laughter, it's really always about the same thing ... connecting hearts and bridging the gaps.

I think Simon and Garfunkel also helped
our understanding of bridge–building
with the lyrics of Bridge Over Troubled Water ...

When you're weary, feeling small,
When tears are in your eyes,
I will dry them all;
I'm on your side, when times get rough
And friends just can't be found,
Like a bridge over troubled water
I will lay me down.

Bridging the Troubled Waters

One of the best things about the idea of bridging troubled waters is that it is a concept that originated with Our Creator. God is always finding ways to build a relationship with us, to create a connection that is sure and steadfast. It was with that intention that He sent His Son into the world to be our bridge to get us home safely again. The ultimate understanding of how love can build a bridge couples the events we celebrate at Christmas and Easter.

We have the example of Jesus, an extraordinary bridge builder, who invites us to be bridges over troubled waters.

We can be the link of forgiveness, the support for the weary, the place where peace may prevail. Where are the gaps in our own lives, the spaces that have fallen between conversations that need to be continued, the misunderstandings that never seem to find a way to be reconciled, the hearts that need to be mended by a gift of love or a warm smile? The opportunity to be a blessing is only a heartbeat away.

You're Not Alone

Have no fear because you won't be the only one on the bridge looking for a way back and forth. You will likely see old friends there who are waiting to reconnect with you, waiting to take your hand again.

We're getting better at social networking. We Twitter and we have friends on Facebook and we get LinkedIn, but couldn't we benefit too from standing in the gaps for each other face to face? Building the bridges keeps us nicely connected so no matter how far away we get, when we're weary and feeling small, we know how to get safely home again.

Blessings to Share ...

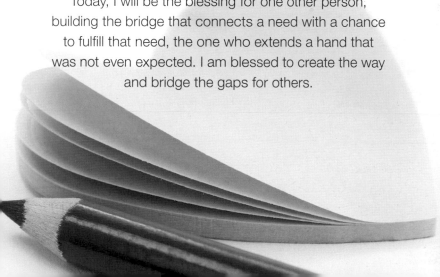

Today, I will be the blessing for one other person, building the bridge that connects a need with a chance to fulfill that need, the one who extends a hand that was not even expected. I am blessed to create the way and bridge the gaps for others.

No man is an island, entire of itself;
every man is a piece of the continent.

John Donne

A Blessing Prayer

Lord, we strive too hard to remain independent, to be an island in a world where the help we need is all around. We limit our own possibilities because we do not dare to look up and receive the gifts of Your blessings, given freely so that we can turn and send the blessing on to someone else. Help us to keep the blessings moving from one person to the next.

Amen.

God has not called us
to see through each other,
but to see each other through.

Anonymous

Blessings and Good Deeds

You generally appreciate it when someone does a good deed for you. When a neighbor stops by with a plate of brownies or mows the grass when you were out of town, you feel grateful. Most of us appreciate those things but often don't recognize the opportunities we have every day to be "good deed doers" ourselves. In fact, the list is almost never-ending of the things we can do for one another. We simply have to choose to see one another through life and not just see through each other.

Acts of God

Nothing shows our willingness to be there for one another more clearly than when natural disasters occur. Suddenly we don't become limited by titles and arbitrary lines of difference, but we become simple people helping other people survive. We become one another's neighbor in the true sense of the word. We are the ones who act on God's behalf — we are His ambassadors bringing order and peace back to one another.

We could recount endless stories of good neighbors; the ones who give canned goods for the food shelter or contribute in some way to all the local charities. Those things become part of our tithe, part of our responsibility to others.

What about those who simply create an opportunity to be a blessing to someone else and never expect anything in return? They don't deduct the deed from their tax ledgers, they don't get an article in the local paper for their kindness, they don't even tell their spouse what they did. They simply do a good deed because they wanted to do so.

When we consider that God does indeed love a cheerful giver, imagine how much more He must love a selfless giver, one who doesn't think twice about the act itself, even if it means going without something important, just to make the deed possible.

Tales of Goodness

The Good Neighbor Guy

A guy in my neighborhood mows lawns. He also does Mr. Fix-It jobs and generally watches out for the neighborhood. Our neighborhood has a lot of elderly single women who don't have resources to pay for landscaping services and yard work. My generous neighbor does it just because he cares, because he wants to help out, and because he wants to answer a need in the best possible way. He took that "love your neighbor" thing seriously. He's a blessing.

The Compassionate Boss

Another guy I know has a small business in Indiana. He has a handful of employees and treats them fairly. One of his employees developed cancer and needed a lot of help. She got to the place where she couldn't work at all. This guy was blessed with the opportunity to buy several condos in Florida.

He bought four of them and remodeled one of them for the woman who worked for him. He gave her the condo to live in for the rest of her life. He gave her a job to oversee his other condos so that she could stay busy and be as active as possible. He's a blessing.

Robin's Cocina

A woman has a small coffee shop and bakery business in a suburb of Costa Rica. She's an American and has adopted this country as her own. When people come into her cocina, they feel happy and blessed. She often donates food to the local homeless shelters. She gives away cakes for family celebrations and charitable organizations that are making meals for shut-ins and other people less fortunate. Her business barely allows her to eke out a living, but she gives to those who need help. She brings a special light to the neighborhood. She's a blessing.

Remember upon the conduct of each depends the fate of all.

Alexander the Great

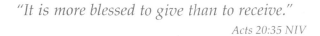

"It is more blessed to give than to receive."

Acts 20:35 NIV

The Generous Landlord

When a woman I know unexpectedly lost her job, she wondered how long she'd be able to continue to pay the rent. She and her daughter were far from home and she knew it would be difficult to even find the money to move them back to her family.

Just one week before the job loss, the woman had made friends with a local businessman. Upon hearing her story, he offered a solution. He was getting ready to vacate his home in the area and was building a new home in another city. He said the woman and her daughter could live in his home and keep it up for him when he was away building the new house. He said they could stay rent free for as long as they wished. He was a blessing.

Blessings Count

The examples mentioned are not unlike the parables we read about in the Bible. They are demonstrations of love and charity from one person to another. They recognize the common bond between us all. They are stories that remind us that we can always count our blessings.

It's unlikely that we could actually count all of our blessings, even if we tried. On any given day, we receive from a generous and loving God gifts beyond measure. We are the recipients of air to breathe, water to drink, and people to love us. We didn't earn any of it. We didn't create any of it and we don't necessarily deserve any of it. We are simply blessed from the unending stream of goodness that emanates from the One who loves us so much.

That is why it is more than a nice thing to be a blessing to another person, it is a calling. It is a reflection of God Himself casting sunlight into the shadows of those in need. You are the ambassador divinely appointed to carry out the blessings, the one who creates the opportunity to shed joy and light into someone else's darkest moments.

What you do, matters. How you give of yourself for the good of other human beings, makes a difference. You become a friend to all of humankind, radiating hope.

William Arthur Ward said, "A true friend knows your weaknesses, but shows you your strengths; feels your fears, but fortifies your faith; sees your anxieties, but frees your spirit; recognizes your disabilities, but emphasizes your possibilities."

That's what it means to be a blessing. That's what makes the difference and causes lives to be changed forever. That's what perpetuates honest to goodness joy and peace of mind.

> If instead of a gem, or even a flower, we should cast
> the gift of a loving thought into the heart of a friend,
> that would be giving as the angels give.
>
> George MacDonald

Today you've been blessed and enriched and nourished. You've become even more aware of how important you are to the great tapestry of life. The threads you weave into the lives of others are pure gold. Some will unravel, some will tear, but most will offer warmth and protection, gifts of infinite joy and blessing. You've been blessed to be a blessing in the same spirit that we read in Genesis 12:1 (MSG) when God talks to Abram and tells him to leave his home for the Promised Land.

God says to him,
"I'll make you a great nation and bless you.
I'll make you famous; you'll be a blessing.

I'll bless those who bless you;
those who curse you I'll curse.
All the families of the Earth will be blessed through you."

Abram obeyed God's leading and because he did so, untold blessings have come to fruition. Today God sends you and me into the world, into the neighborhood, wherever we go to pass on the blessing, to share it with everyone we meet. Our forefathers made it a habit to bless their children and it was considered a great favor when they did so. A friend of mine carries on that tradition with his own children and though they are now grown, he continues to call them often and bless them again. They have found favor in such a blessing.

We lift each other up, we light the way, we make it possible for others to be blessed through the work we do. We are the blessing and we owe it to our families, our friends, and our neighbors to pass the blessing on. As the saying goes, when we truly count our blessings, we have no time left to count our sorrows.

Blessings to Share ...

Today, I will offer **a blessing** to someone in my family, to someone in my neighborhood and to someone who is a complete stranger. I will be blessed in return with **peace** and **humble joy.**

Thanks
for the blessing you are
to everyone who knows you.
Your light will shine
for eternity.